One of the Lucky Ones

Rescued by the Kindertransport

One of the Lucky Ones

Rescued by the Kindertransport

Bob Rosner

Interviewed by David Turner, August 2005

THE HOLOCAUST CENTRE

One of the Lucky Ones
Rescued by the Kindertransport
Bob Rosner
Interviewed by David Turner, August 2005

Published in Great Britain by
The Holocaust Centre
in association with The Aegis Trust
Laxton, Newark,
Nottinghamshire, NG 22 0PA
UK

British Library Catalogue in Publication Data
A catalogue record for this book is available from the British Library

ISBN 09543001-9-X
978-0-9543001-9-7

Cover photo: Bob, aged 8, photographed on the day before he left for England.

Dedicated to

the Mayerhofer family

and all those

who – often at great personal risk –

protected, sheltered and saved the lives

of my parents

The Interview

David Turner (DT): I'm here in Hessle, just west of Hull, in the home of Bob Rosner. Bob was not brought up here in England. I'm going to invite him to tell you something about his origins.

Bob Rosner (BR): I was born Robert Hans Rosner in Vienna on 22 September 1930. My father was Jewish;[1] my mother had been Catholic, but had become Jewish;[2] and I had an elder sister,[3] who was four years older than me. That completed our family. We lived in the centre of Vienna, in the First District;[4] and throughout my early Austrian life, we lived in a flat which appeared to me to be very similar to that occupied by everyone else living in the centre of Vienna. To this day people still live in flats and it is only on the outskirts of Vienna that people live in houses.

DT: Could you tell us something about your parents' background: what your father's occupation was and how long he had lived in Vienna?

BR: My father had been born in what was then the Austrian part of Poland, referred to by German-speakers as *Schlesien*. He was born in a place called Bielitz,[5] near Krakow, and was brought up there as a young man, until he was old enough (and had passed some academic qualifications) for his father to send him to be educated at the University of Vienna, where he studied medicine. He subsequently became a well-known specialist in Vienna, working at several clinics and hospitals, and his particular field was skin and venereal diseases (*Haut- und Geschlechtskrankheiten*).[6]

DT: And how would you estimate your parents' level of assimilation into Viennese life?

BR: I would say their assimilation into Viennese life was complete. My parents had some Jewish friends, whom we met from time to time. Most of our friends were not Jewish. Like most other Jewish families in German-speaking lands, both in Germany and Austria, we all thought of ourselves as being Austrians who happened to be Jewish, rather than Jewish people who had somehow settled in Austria. We lived the same sort of life, ate the same sort of food, wore the same sort of clothes, conducted the normal kind of practices and joined the same sort of institutions.

I suppose it's true to say that normal Jewish people in Austria, as in Germany, had assimilated very well. They knew they were Jewish and didn't make any special secret or fancy ideas about it. But, by and large, they conducted themselves like all the other citizens of the country. Naturally, on special holy days like Yom Kippur, the Day of Atonement, and various other religious occasions, they made a practice of going to the synagogue.

There was a small group of very Orthodox Jews in Vienna who looked different from the others because the men tended to wear black hats. They went to the synagogue every week, more than once, ate kosher food and tended to have friends who were like them. They were not so well assimilated, but as far as I could tell, they also conducted a normal sort of professional and business life.

DT: And could you tell us something about your schooling in Vienna? Which school did you go to?

BR: It was the Catholic *Volksschule der Schotten* and, as far as I could tell, it was like any other local junior school. Because we were in the centre of Vienna, the chances are that it was academically of a somewhat higher standard than out in the sticks.[7] Vienna itself was really the only thoroughly developed urban centre in Austria. The other towns tended to be smaller and less developed. There was also a great political difference, because

Vienna, which was a vast city of several million – I think two million in a country of only about ten million – was Socialist and had been left-wing ever since the First World War. All the rest of Austria was right-wing, so there was a great political difference.

Our school was part of the urban district education system. I enjoyed going to school and made lots of friends there. It was within walking distance from where we lived and that's how I met most of my friends, who also lived in flats and were a short public transport or walking distance from school. And I think most, if not every one of the kids in my class, had previously been to a Kindergarten school – they were more like schools than play schools. Very young children were actually required to do a little bit of academically productive work, like learning to speak and write the language properly. So by the time we got to the junior school, everybody could read and write quite well.

DT: As far as you know, was your father very politically aware or even politically active?

BR: My father was politically aware, but he was not politically active. He was a doctor from top to toe and that was his life. He really loved it; he was intrigued by medical problems. He made a name for himself in the 1920s by jointly producing an internationally published paper for dealing with syphilis by giving people malaria treatment. It was called 'Trépol', and in the 1920s he and a colleague discovered that in very severe syphilis cases, by giving carefully proportioned malaria effectively to patients, they could stop them dying. The malaria, with its high temperature, tended to kill the virus or whatever, the disease instead of the patient.[8]

DT: So he was first and foremost a doctor, but in the family was there an awareness of some of the big political events in the 1930s? I'm thinking, for example, of the murder of the Austrian Chancellor, Engelbert Dollfuss.[9]

BR: Dollfuss, yes. This was known about and discussed. Of course, as a boy of seven or eight at the time, there was a limit to my awareness of these events. But my father was a Social Democrat and as such he understood the immediate threat of the combined military and Austrian-Nazi – that is Fascist – activity which was going on and beginning to dominate life.

I should perhaps point out from a political point of view that Vienna may well have been the first place in the world to have social housing on a massive scale. In the 1920s and 30s, many hundreds of so-called 'workers' flats' were built. These were built to what was then a high standard of accommodation, combined with central heating facilities and central laundry, not to mention shops and so on.[10] All of this was very much hated and disliked by the right-wing people, who didn't believe in this sort of thing.

Vienna also had a lot of trade unionists who were very much hated by the right-wing. So there developed what I perhaps mistakenly referred to as 'Austrian Nazis' who were really Fascists; they were extreme right-wing. It was a combination of the military, very right-wing politicians and, as everyone believed, the Church. To this day, the right-wing in Austria are referred to as the 'Blacks' because that was the colour of the priest's gown. It is now a misnomer and a nonsense. And the left-wing Social Democrats were referred to as the 'Reds' because that was the colour of the Communist flag.

DT: Within your family, were these social issues, such as the housing and political developments, talked about?

BR: They were talked about. But as far as I know, none of the family were members of a political party and they were not activists.

DT: So at what stage did you become aware of the political threats, and particularly the antisemitism?

BR: Real awareness happened from the moment the *Anschluss* took place in 1938, when the citizens of Austria voted 90+ per cent to join the Nazi German *Reich*. The *Anschluss* took place,[11] and very quickly antisemitism of a very fierce and aggressive kind began to hurt every single Jew in the place.

I became very aware of the significance of what was happening because within days of the *Anschluss* and the German Nazi authorities taking control of the Austrian state, a crudely constructed white-painted bench appeared at the front of our classroom, labelled '*Für Juden*'. That was where I and another unfortunate youth had to sit, exposed as being special and different at the front of the class. And at that moment all our friends in the classroom stopped speaking to us; they all stopped playing and mixing with us. I remember that as a very strange and traumatic experience – suddenly all the friends we'd been playing with gathered together in the far corner of the classroom and they might talk about us, point at us, sneer or laugh at us, but they no longer wanted to be with us.

DT: And that was without exception?

BR: Yes, without exception. The situation didn't last very long because after a week or two we were thrown out of the school, as happened to most Jewish children in most schools. Then we were made to go to a special school created by the new Nazi authorities, which was also quite close to where I lived in the centre of Vienna.[12] It was peopled entirely by Jewish pupils who had been thrown out of the schools they previously attended, and staffed entirely by Jewish teachers who had been thrown out of their jobs at other schools. The only exception was the Head, who was a proper uniform-wearing Stormtrooper, an SA [*Sturmabteilung*] man in a brown uniform with highly polished boots and swastika armband, of course; and he was the guy who ran this institution. Heaven knows what he knew about schooling, but he was good at time-tabling, because from the very first day there, he arranged for our school to finish at least a quarter of an hour later than the big boys' school round the corner. So they had time to come and wait at our school entrance and beat the hell out of us as we left. So every single day we got used to being tripped up, spat on, beaten up, dragged round the corner and kicked, just because we were Jewish.

DT: You had an older sister who presumably by that time had gone to another school. Did she have a similar experience?

BR: My sister's experience wasn't the same. She wasn't thrown out of a class, but she was discriminated against, hassled and harassed, and the teachers would point her out as an evil student in the class. She wasn't thrown out of the school, but she had the same experience as I did of seeing people beaten up and thrown into the backs of lorries by uniformed Nazis or people in authority on her way to and from school – and her journey was longer than mine.

She had started on what we would call a grammar-school type of education. She had a particular memory of the morning after *Kristallnacht* [The Night of Broken Glass],[13] the night when the Nazis really set about burning and destroying synagogues and other Jewish property. They dislodged, looted and generally had a shot at destroying Jewish-owned shops and industry – mostly shops. We all saw the shops owned by Jewish families, which we might have known in advance of course, with painted signs, saying, 'This is a Jewish outfit. Don't shop here.' But more often, the windows were also smashed and the contents looted. That was quite a common sight.

What was also very common in Vienna was that, over and over again, Jews were pulled out of wherever they were living and made to scrub the streets with antiseptic. This provided great entertainment for the others. In their view, these rotten Jews with their filthy, verminous feet had sullied the pavements of Vienna and were finally getting their comeuppance and being made to scrub them clean. This attracted great crowds. Great cheers would go up when somebody kicked a bucket over, so the Jews were kneeling in the liquid of course. And that happened over and over again, a thousand times.

DT: Did that happen to Jews of all social classes?

BR: Yes, that was immaterial.

DT: Did anything like that happen to your parents?

BR: My parents didn't have to do this, but immediately across the street from where we lived there were two ladies, probably in their thirties, who ran a bookshop. I remember them being pulled out and made to scrub the streets. We could see it from our window.

I should say, of course, that we as a family were thrown out of our flat. Fortunately, my father was on very good terms with the person responsible for the house, and through a friend with the same job in a nearby block of flats, this concierge was able to arrange for us to live there in an empty flat on a temporary basis. This kind concierge also arranged to use his pass key to let my parents back into our flat on a Sunday, so they could get some of their things that hadn't been stolen. That was the sort of society I was now living in.

DT: And was your father's work at the clinic affected at all by this at this stage?

BR: Yes, my father lost all his jobs. Jews couldn't work in clinics and hospitals and so on. And each one of the different institutions in turn had to write to him. Usually they were clearly very sad to write and issue the letters, which all said they didn't want his services any longer. They mostly managed to work in some words to the effect that he'd been super as a doctor, but it meant that he lost all his jobs.

DT: At what stage, then, did it become apparent to your parents that life was in danger and that you ought if possible to move away?

BR: I think it was at *Kristallnacht* when there was an enormous amount of destruction. Quite a few people were killed, a great many people were in prison, people were thrown out of flats and things were looted, stolen, and so on. This was in 1938. It was also made clear to my parents that they were not allowed to have passports. The Nazis varied in their history on this: on some occasions they allowed Jews to have passports and in fact encouraged them to leave; at other times they refused to issue them with documents. And my parents were concerned when they refused to let them have documents. They couldn't effectively travel out of Austria.

They also saw and learnt what was happening to other people, besides what had happened within our family. What none of us could avoid was that every single radio bulletin (there was no television of course), every single issue of every newspaper was absolutely full of big items about these 'rotten Jews', how the 'rotten Jews' had to be dealt with, how they were preventing the good Aryan people of Austria from making progress, getting promotion, making money and finding good employment. All of this was happening because these 'rotten, filthy, verminous, insect-like Jewish people' were effectively sapping the body economic and body politic of Austria with their viciousness and nastiness.

This was reinforced by the fact that at every major street crossing, as I recall, five- or six-metre high posters appeared, usually depicting a grotesque, Shylock-like character with a big figure-six nose, doing unmentionable things to little girls or little boys, or perhaps only stealing, putting his hand into somebody's handbag or pocket.

DT: So did your parents then decide that you and your sister ought, if possible, to leave?

BR: They were desperate to find ways of protecting us. I recall that my father was visited by a friend of his, who wasn't Jewish but had just been a couple of months in one of the early concentration camps because he was a trade unionist. I remember the friend looking very bad and hearing him tell my father how he had witnessed the authorities there nailing a man up in a plywood crate with hundreds of four- and six-inch nails, then forcing the prisoners to roll the crate around the parade ground until the screaming stopped. That was the sort of world I now inhabited and my parents were desperate to try and protect their kids.

At that juncture the *Kindertransport* organization opened an office in Vienna. It was set up by a combination of some Jewish agencies in the UK, the Society of Friends (Quakers) in the UK and the British Red Cross in order to try and save children like me, whose lives were thought to be at risk. They had previously arranged with the British Government that it would permit immigration of such children on certain provisos: first of all, that they had access to or could bring with them £50 or its equivalent – a lot of money in 1938-39; secondly, that they got themselves exit documentation, which was, of course, necessary to leave the country; thirdly, and most importantly, that they found a host, a person, an institution or a school, who would take total responsibility for the bringing up of that child, so that it would never become a charge on the state.

Now my father wondered how to use this organization and he remembered that he knew a young girl who was working as an au pair in London. He wrote to this girl, outlining the circumstances, and asked her if she could possibly find someone who might be willing to take all liability and responsibility for bringing up my sister, who at that stage, four years older than me, was about 12. This girl in London had a boyfriend who was a commercial traveller in the greengrocery world, and he said, "Let's put an advert in the specialist press." And so they put an advert in something like the *Greengrocers Times*. A fruiterer and greengrocer on Anlaby High Road in Hull responded,[14] saying that he had a daughter of similar age to my sister and he would take full responsibility for my sister. So my father had found protection in England for his daughter.

He then went back to the *Kindertransport* organization and asked if there was any chance whatever of finding someone not too far away, where he could send the boy. Well, in those days, in Hull as in many other towns of Great Britain, there was a so-called refugee committee whose purpose was specifically to find hosts and homes for such people as me. And I was lucky enough to be picked out of the hat, as it were, by one of the members of the committee, a wonderful person called Leo Schultz,[15] who decided that he could bring me up. He also had a son of his own who was very nearly my age.[16] And that's how I became a *Kindertransportee*.

DT: In a sense we've jumped ahead a little bit, but what I also wondered was whether your parents discussed all these arrangements with the two of you before you began arrangements?

BR: Yes, pretty well as soon as they had decided to find protectors in this manner, they talked to us about it. They didn't pretend that we were being sent on holiday or anything like that. That did happen with many parents. Really, perhaps the greatest victims of the situation were the parents. You can imagine the difficulties, which are every parent's nightmare: having to consider sending their daughter or son to some strange, unknown country to be protected and brought up. How can you bring yourself to tear yourself from your children? Sadly, of course, those who couldn't bring themselves to do this were murdered, all of them. The *Kindertransport* organization, which brought me to England, brought a total of nearly 10,000 children to Great Britain. There were more than 1.5 million such children murdered by the Nazis. So this 10,000, of which I was lucky enough to be one, is a tiny, tiny proportion.

DT: Yes. And what were your feelings about this before it happened? Was there an internal struggle?

BR: There was certainly an internal struggle. In my case, it was combined with a total lack of understanding of what I might be going to. I had no idea what things might be like in England. But I think that perhaps goes for every one of the *Kindertransportees*. We had no idea of what sort of world we were going to. Nobody was able to tell us about cultural things, about food or language, or really properly about anything. The easiest thing really for those who were old enough would be to learn a few words of English. I'm afraid I didn't learn any words of English before I came.

DT: Had your sister learnt any?

BR: My sister had learnt the odd word or two, but in practice it didn't amount to much.

DT: We've got to the point where arrangements have been made for this *Kindertransport*. I wonder if you could tell us a little bit about the mechanics of this and your feelings as you embarked on this journey into the unknown?

BR: It *was* a journey into the unknown. I was just under nine years old and I left Vienna on 20 June 1939. I had no conception of what the end station, the terminus, might consist of. I didn't know anything about England really and, of course, I couldn't speak English. But I also had no conception of what kind of journey it might be.

I think that in all cases it was a very difficult thing for people to decide what things they might put into their small suitcase or bag. I still have here a silver spoon. My parents decided that I should have something to remind me of my home. They perhaps knew that the probability of us meeting again was very small and they had a knife, fork and spoon engraved with my name, Robert, and this is what remains. But consider the problem. How do you as a young person, how do you as a parent, decide what to put in one small case or bag? Do you put in things to do with washing and cleaning? Do you put in clothes? Toys? Do you put in mementos of home maybe? What do you exclude? It's a great problem, and it was a great problem for all of us. I think that at the finish it was mostly clothing.

The fact is that our parents were not allowed to actually say goodbye to us at the railway station. They had to stay outside because they were Jewish. Now on different occasions that rule was relaxed and I've met several people from Vienna whose parents were allowed onto the station. But in my case they were not, so we had to say our goodbyes outside. My parents went to a lot of trouble to explain and tell my sister that she must look after me. My sister, by this time aged 13, was told how important it was to look after me, who was coming up for nine. And she was enjoined to make sure that I was well and properly looked after – quite an important sort of load to give to a 13-year-old child, going into the unknown.

I felt pretty lousy, of course, at being separated from my parents. There was a feeling of adventure in going off into the unknown, because I knew that the life surrounding me was difficult, dangerous and harassing. I wasn't sure that all of this would disappear and now I would find something much better, but of course I hoped and expected to do so. I can remember little of the actual train journey, except that the train was stopped once or twice for uniformed folks to get on and go through all the luggage, of course, take whatever they wanted and generally harass and intimidate the young people. My only memory of that train journey is that it was kind of grey. But I do seem to recall the train stopping after it crossed the Dutch border and the sun shining; and in the sunshine there were a lot of nice ladies who were serving us with coffee, tea, biscuits, chocolate, who would smile, pat us on the head, put their arms round us and generally make us feel that, at least in that part of the world, we were not verminous insects to be done away with.

DT: Had the route taken you through Germany to the Dutch border?

BR: Yes.

DT: And were you accompanied at all by any adults?

BR: There was somebody from the *Kindertransport* organization, I can't remember who it was. I don't remember anything about the ship across from the Hook of Holland to Harwich, but of course I do remember landing on a grey, drizzly morning at Harwich and being met in a transit shed by the people who became my guardian and my sister's guardian. My sister's guardian, the fruit and vegetable trader, actually had a car,[17] which not everyone did in 1939. And he had arranged to come all the way down to Harwich by car to bring my guardian, who didn't have a car, to meet the children. And that's how we arrived on 'Mars'.

DT: Listening to you now, no one would detect that you had spoken anything but English all your life. Do you remember anything about the process by which you acquired English and lost your Viennese?

BR: Well, I spoke no English and this made life very difficult indeed because naturally the two fellows who had picked us up kept trying to talk to us. We understood not a word. I said that we had arrived on Mars, as it were, because everything was totally different from what we had left. The clothes that people wore were different; the fields in the countryside looked different; it looked as if everybody lived in little houses. Where I came from nobody lived in little houses; everybody lived in flats. The trains were different; the buses and cars looked quite different, drove on a different side of the road, and so on. When we stopped to use toilets and have a cup of tea, we were offered this grotesque kind of tea and the snacks were not very palatable. But it was obvious that the two people who had met us, who became our guardians, were dying to be friendly, helpful and welcoming. But there was no language communication.

Now when I arrived at my new home, I found that my hosts, my guardian, my uncle Leo and auntie Kitty,[18] and my foster brother Lionel, as I got to know them, were mad keen for me to learn English. And they had devised many, many ways of helping me to do this. The first thing was that I was immediately, the very next day, sent to school with my foster brother. I went to Bricknell Avenue Junior School in Hull, where a young teacher, who had learnt some German during her training college course, was given one hour one-to-one with me to start teaching me English. Even that wasn't a straightforward experience. I can still recall this very pleasant young lady trying to help me learn some English as I heard out of the corner of my ear, as it were, young kids in a nearby classroom reciting tables. And I discovered that here on 'Mars', they didn't stop at ten-times-ten. This was absolutely incredible. Why were they going on to eleven-times and twelve-times? I hadn't yet cottoned on to the duodecimal currency system. But I had this English-language tuition every day for a number of weeks at school.

It was, of course, a bright idea of my foster parents to insist on sending me directly to school with their son, Lionel. I also discovered that from the word go, Lionel wanted to be my ally. Every fight in the playground, he stood alongside me, and it was the two of us against the rest. So I realized that there was a loyalty from my guardian's son immediately. But perhaps the most significant way for me to learn English and about English ways was that my guardians encouraged all their neighbours from the terrace of houses where we lived to visit in the evenings and try and engage me in slow but purposeful English conversation. Quite a few did that, so that nearly every night there were two or three neighbours coming in to see me and help me.

I was also sent out to play in the street after school and at weekends, and that was much more difficult because I understood nothing about the street games. I'd never heard of cricket. I tried to sit on the stumps and the kids didn't really want me! I'd never heard anything about people playing marbles in the gutter, up against the edge of the pavement, which they all did; and I'd never seen people on roller skates. All of this was a novelty and something I couldn't really cotton on to, and because I couldn't speak the language and wore outlandish clothes, the kids in the street weren't really very keen on me. Lionel tried hard to introduce me to them, but I was too outlandish, I think.

Tied up with that was an extraordinary, difficult and intimate problem that I came across. We lived in a mid-terrace house,[19] which had an entrance from the street, with a staircase straight upstairs to a bathroom and two bedrooms. You turned straight into the living room and at the back of the living room was the kitchen. Then across an open court there was a coalhouse and WC. All of this was shown to me, painstakingly, but the explanations had been in English, so I'd understood nothing. And the second and third explanations didn't help either.

Now, for a boy, urinating is not such a terrible problem, but sooner or later you have to do something else. And I found I didn't know where the toilet was. So the first night, after all the trauma of the journey, meeting all these people and coming up to Yorkshire, I waited until everyone else was asleep, then I tiptoed downstairs to try and find this wretched toilet. It was dark by then and I discovered that I couldn't switch the light on, because where I came from all light switches were turned. I'd never come across light switches that you flicked up and down, so I couldn't turn the light on. In the dark, I stumbled around the living room, the kitchen and so on and found nothing. But at the back of the kitchen corner my hand did meet a switch I could turn. I turned it, nothing happened and I forgot about it – which meant that in the morning the kitchen was full of acrid smoke because I had turned on the latest gadget in the kitchen, a small electric clothes boiler which had some dirty washing in it.

Anyhow, two or three days of this new 'Martian' living led to me having a high temperature because I hadn't been to the toilet properly. My guardians were able to contact a local immigrant German doctor,[20] who came to see me, understood the problem, showed me where the toilet was and prescribed something to make me go. That was it; I was OK from then on.

And it was immediately after that, perhaps in the flush of success, that I put on my particular Austrian clothing to come down to breakfast – a green Austrian-type jacket and leather pants. Now I don't know how it happened, but the kids in the street discovered that these leather pants of mine were proof against airgun pellets! That was a revolutionary event in my assimilation down that street because from being an outlandish, unwelcome interloper, I suddenly became a hero. And these kids insisted on taking me to all the reachable neighbouring streets where I had to bend over and demonstrate the magical properties of my leather pants. So that's how I became one of the lads in the street. And, of course, as soon as I had a few words of English at my command, they would help by sending me to the corner shop for things like 'elbow grease' or 'strap oil', which not only helped improve my English, but helped me develop a keenly active mind.[21]

DT: And an English sense of humour.

BR: And an English sense of humour, yes.

DT: In all this time were you in regular contact with your sister?

BR: I met my sister very occasionally. She lived at the other end of Hull, but I met her occasionally. My sister really had less than two years at school[22] because people left school at 14 then. And as a near-13-year-old, she had limited experience. By the time she left school, the war was on, of course, and she finished up being a member of the Land Army. She worked in the Land Army throughout the war.

DT: Do you remember at all, when you were in contact with your sister, whether you always spoke German together, or did a transfer take place at some stage and you felt more at home speaking English?

BR: I think the transfer took place pretty quickly because we were both very keen to demonstrate our command of a new language. It was, of course, essential for every possible purpose. And we had no love for German. The last thing we wanted to do was speak German. In my case, it took me no more than about two years to forget German.

DT: Could you tell us a little about your schooling here and how different it was from what you'd been used to?

BR: Well, because of the persistent and intelligent direction of my guardians, academically my education became very good. I was encouraged not only to learn English, but actually to use it to read – and the house was full of useful books. I was also encouraged to talk about educational matters with my foster parents. All of this, together with the fact that the junior school which I attended must have been very good, led to me being able to pass my scholarship exam as it was called then, the 11+ examination, which qualified me for a place at grammar school or a grammar-school type of secondary education. I think the junior school must have been pretty good because I remember learning about algebra before I ever went to secondary school. I'm not by nature a mathematical sort of person, but at secondary school, I found in the first year that I was one of a very small number of people who had been introduced to algebra.

I went to a kind of grammar school called Kingston High School, noted in the history books as the school that Amy Johnson[23] went to in her youth, when it had a different name.[24] The school's ethos was to encourage all pupils to make the most of every talent. Everyone was taught not to be discouraged by being a poor scholar in a particular sphere; just because you weren't picked as the captain of cricket, it shouldn't mean that you didn't enjoy playing cricket. And the same would apply to French or German, for instance. As it happened, by the time I got to Kingston High School, the war was well on its way and bombing was a regular event in Hull. German was no longer taught at the school and many of the teachers were away fighting elsewhere. So what had been very great choices of curricula no longer existed. But I was very pleased immediately to feel and become part of the fellowship of the pupils of the school. I made lots of friends; nobody discriminated against me because I was Jewish; nobody questioned or asked me about any such matters... only very rarely. They all knew that I came from Vienna and that I was looked after by my foster parents, my guardians. But it didn't seem to make any difference to how anyone behaved to me. It didn't seem to make it necessary for me to adapt how I behaved to other people. So I enjoyed the fellowship of this new school.

DT: You mentioned that Hull was quite heavily bombed during the war. Did it ever seem to you that you had escaped from one kind of danger and were exposed to another?

BR: I realized the danger, but only from the point of view of a nine-, ten- or eleven-year-old at first. Young children aren't as sensitive to the dangers as adults because the adventure is quite important. In Hull we had the advantage of Anderson shelters[25] in the garden, and those who didn't have them in the garden, had the advantage of other shelters nearby. Largely because of the leadership of my guardian, who was chairman of the Finance Committee, the local authority in Hull was committed to the building of shelters throughout the city, long before the Government authorized such spending.[26] And this meant that in Hull, in spite of being very, very heavily bombed, the casualty rate was very low.

Now, one of the things that immediately impinged on my life was in the street games. I told you that on 'Mars' I was surprised to discover that they played this funny game of marbles. Well, I have to tell you that within a few experiences of real bombing by German aircraft, the kids stopped playing with marbles and started playing a similar game with bits of shrapnel and bomb splinters. All the boys I knew became skilled at devising different sorts of throwing systems when employing the small bits of shrapnel which came from anti-aircraft shells that were very heavy steel; the much bigger pieces of ragged steel which came from actual bombs and were irregular shapes; and the much bigger, even more irregular, twisted pieces of aluminium, which came from so-called parachute mines. Boys would walk to and from school carrying little boxes or bags with all these different sorts of splinters in, and they would play, shying these along the pavement edge, just as they had done before with marbles. Very strange.

I was briefly evacuated to Bingley in the West Riding, together with a large contingent from my school. We stayed there as evacuees with local families and went to school at the local Bingley Grammar School, where they gave up some of their classrooms for some of our teachers to teach us in our way. That didn't last for very long and we came back to Hull. When Hull was bombed, I became quite used to sleeping in the shelter. Our Anderson shelter, like most of our neighbours', was eventually concreted over and adapted to eliminate damp by great big pits being dug outside to take surface water. Then bunks were built in, so one could sleep there, and an electric cable was dragged across from the house, so one could have light. Because my guardians were always busy in civil defence roles whenever there was an air raid, my foster brother and I were used to sleeping in those bunks, often with some other older boy from the neighbouring street sent to keep us company.

DT: Now, should we move forward a little bit to the rest of your education? Could you tell us how you succeeded there and what you went on to do?

BR: Well, I never thought of myself as being academically very successful, but it turned out that I was at least very lucky. When I was 16, or just before I was 16, I was encouraged to stay on at school to go into the sixth form because it was thought I might pass matriculation, the School Certificate. And, with my guardian's considerable help and advice, I did manage to do well enough for that purpose.

I can still remember that I was very bad at French, and it was the only foreign language that I could take. I was taught by a very good French teacher called Miss DeVelling.[27] One day, I had managed to buy a Sally Lunn [a tea cake], which I was sharing with a fellow pupil by passing him a piece across the aisle, when she turned round from the blackboard, saw what I was doing and threw me, the other boy and another three boys out of the class. Standing out in the corridor, we were then told we were holding up the progress of the rest of the class and we shouldn't go back into French. As it happened, that very month, a French teacher had been invalided out of the Air Force after being wounded, and sent back to the school.[28] He had nothing to do, so they gave him the five of us for French, the crucial year before our School Certificate examination. And I have to say that every one of the five of us passed. We all got a credit. Many of the others didn't, so he must have been a super teacher.

But I also recall that my guardian gave me some excellent advice. Knowing that I was weak in French, he said, "You know, examinations, as you will learn, are just like games of football. There are rules which you must follow, and you have to learn how to work within these rules. Among these rules is that in French exams most marks are awarded for an essay. You have to learn to produce a French essay." He continued, "Because you're so weak, why don't you learn a piece of French from one of your textbooks that you can use under different headings?" And I thought, "What a wonderful idea!" So I learnt a piece about a farm: "The sun came up, the cock crew, the cows went to be milked," and so on. I learnt this by heart and sure enough, when the exam came along, there was this great long list of topics to write an essay about. I went straight for this, but couldn't find any topic about farms, about cows or a cock crowing. Then suddenly I spotted it. It said: "My last holiday". So all I had to do was construct the words, "I spent my last holiday on a farm," then I regurgitated this stuff. Anyway, one way or another, I managed to get a credit in French among other things, and so I went into the sixth form.

At the age of 16, of course, I had to start signing on at the police station as an alien. I went regularly to sign on although I was a schoolboy, and through that I came to know a friendly policeman who was an Assistant Chief Constable. He joined forces with my headmaster[29] and one of the local members of Parliament[30] to petition the Home Office to allow me to apply for naturalization, although I was too young at the time. I applied and was eventually granted British citizenship in 1947.

As soon as I became a British citizen of course, the first thing I did was sign on for military service, because I thought that was the most direct way of making a payback to this new society that I'd joined. Perhaps I should say that in historical terms, there were three miraculous things that happened to me in 1947. The first one of these I will mention, although it's not in sequence, was an academic one. Miraculously, I was encouraged to take a two-day examination and was actually awarded a major award scholarship – a scholarship to study at university. This enabled me to go and study architecture at Durham University. It was a total surprise to me and I think to everyone else, but it was a miracle that happened to me at that time.

The other two miraculous things were that at the end of 1946 or beginning of 1947, I discovered that my parents in Austria had survived the Holocaust in Europe. They had survived because my father's best friend and one or two other people had hidden and protected them through all those long years. They had survived. It took them more than a year for us to be in contact because they were in the Russian zone of Vienna, and contact between the Russian zone and the rest was very difficult, to say the least. But we discovered they were alive. So that was another miracle. And then the third miracle was that I became a British citizen. So a group of three 1947 miracles for me: I discovered that my parents were alive; getting a university scholarship; and becoming a naturalized British citizen.

DT: Could we, then, go back for a little while to the second of these miracles: discovering that your parents were alive, because this in some ways seems most remarkable. Had you had any word from them at all since you arrived in England?

BR: No. There had been one exchange of letters. I wrote in June 1939 and there was one exchange of letters between my parents and my guardians before the beginning of the war. That's all. I had no reason to believe they were alive. And they, of course, had no idea what had happened to me. But their survival is a true, genuine miracle, which I would call a miracle of humanity.

DT: How did you get to learn of this?

BR: My parents eventually managed to talk to a British officer in Vienna. They told him who they were, that they had children here in England and would like to make contact. This guy, of course, didn't know what on earth was going on and thought it a bit of a nuisance, but he evidently went to the British and sent off some kind of message via the post office. At about the same time, my guardian knew a member of the House of Commons, Mrs Lucy Middleton,[31] a Labour MP who was going on a mission to have a look at post-war Vienna. She went on this mission armed with the last-known address of my parents, having been asked to find out what had happened to them.

So my parents managed to talk to a British soldier outside the Russian zone and Lucy Middleton set off for this mission to Vienna. She immediately went to the British army in Vienna with her information, the last-known address of my parents, and asked them to check and see what had happened to my parents. At that time in Vienna, as in the centre of Berlin, there were four-party military police patrols every day. A Russian, an American, a French and a British member of the military police would drive a jeep around. They took it in turns to drive in each another's territory and they got to be able to communicate with each other a little. One day, this scrap of information was given to the British member of one of these regular security tours, and he asked them to stop if they could find the address. And they found the address. My parents were actually found at the same address as I had last lived in in 1939. An incredible miracle.

DT: It is. So could you tell us how that came about?

BR: From 1939 to 1943, my parents lived only by the protection of people who were full of enough humanity to want to save them – at total risk of their own lives. My mother came from a Catholic family and had converted to become Jewish. And therefore she had sisters who were Aryan, proper Aryan, and able to live as much of a normal life as it was possible to do under the Nazis. One of these, Maria,[32] was a particularly able administrator and director of a big company in Vienna. It had been stolen from a Jew who was thrown out in 1938 and he had arranged for the subsequent Nazi owners to make her the administrative director. So she had a top job throughout the war, which not only paid her well, but gave her all sorts of advantages. For instance, she was often able to use a car and she also had access to all kinds of means of assisting her sister, my mother, and her husband. She started off by securing for them all the things that hadn't been stolen, including a particular locket of my mother's which is still in existence, and books of my father's.

She was also able to arrange for them to hide in a variety of hiding places around Vienna. The normal blocks of flats there had one large divided roof space, with its own lock and key and two windows, to dry washing. Each normal flat also had a very large cellar, not just for keeping coal, but also for storing other things. So for every flat in every block of flats, there were at least two spaces that could be used as hiding places by people like my parents. Several people were prepared to make these sorts of facilities available to my parents. Another person, who had a country house on the outskirts of Vienna, had what he called a 'wine cellar', which was really a timber building in which he stored wine, where he also protected and kept my parents for a while.

But the most significant event that truly, and to everyone's knowledge, saved their lives came from the actions of the man who had been my father's best friend when he was a college student learning medicine. His best friend, Viktor Mayerhofer,[33] had gone on to be a vet, a country vet in a place out in the sticks called Böheimkirchen,[34] where he became a regionally very well known vet. Besides living in the biggest house in this village, he also had what he called a vegetable garden, which was really a fenced-off smallholding, located quite apart from any other buildings or people on the lower slopes of the local mountain. It also had a well and a substantial timber building.

Early on in 1943, this courageous individual took a horse and cart to where he knew my parents were hiding in Vienna, put them on the back of this rully[35] and said that he would save their lives if he could. He transported them about 50 kilometres to this place Böheimkirchen[36] and at night took them up into this timber building, telling them to use the well and vegetables, but only at night in the dark, and otherwise not to stick their noses out of the door. He would send rations up the hill as and when he could.[37] And you may imagine that as a country vet, he would have rather more rations than most. That's how he secured the survival of my parents for two years, because 1943 was the year when virtually every last remaining Jew in the Vienna area was sent to Auschwitz or a similar industrial killing place.

So that's how my parents survived until 1945, towards the end of the war, when the first Allied troops into that part of Austria were a Russian artillery battery. My father had been born in the Austrian part of Poland and had therefore learnt some words of Russian then. The Russian artillery battery that came up the hill had suffered a lot of casualties and only had two guns left. My father made himself known to the boy in charge of these guns, who immediately roped them in as supernumeraries, my mother as scavenger and cook and my father as sanitary orderly. And he said to my parents, "You come with me. If we make it alive to the end of the war, I'll make sure you have somewhere to live" – no idle boast because half of Europe was living in holes in the ground then.

Anyhow, when the war ended in 1945, this boy was able to put his guns actually in the street where I had last lived in Vienna. He installed my parents on the third floor of the building that I had last lived in. The top two or three floors had been destroyed during the fighting. So on what we would call VE Day, my parents finished up living on Russian rations on the third floor of a partially derelict building that I had inhabited in 1939. Amazing. It took a long, long time to communicate at all with them because the Russian zone was impenetrable to the rest of the world. Russian soldiers throughout the frontier of the Russian zone were changed every two months or so, so they should never get to know the capitalists. There was practically no transport. But eventually, in the centre of Vienna, these things changed and there was some transport and you could move from one zone to the other.

DT: I understand that you were eventually able to be reunited with your parents. Could you tell us how that came about?

BR: First it was possible for me to meet my father by bringing him over to the UK. This was done through the auspices of the police. It happened that my father, a skin specialist, was of interest to the Assistant Chief

Constable in Hull who had been such a great help to me regarding my citizenship. He had a daughter with a most awful disfigured face and through the Home Office system, he arranged for my father to come to this country for special treatment of his daughter. That's how I came to meet my father after the war. He came and spent a couple of days in Hull, met this young lady and went back again. And of course he also met my sister. Then the four of us – my father, mother, sister and I – had a meeting in the American zone of Austria a couple of years later.

DT: I wonder if you could tell us a little bit about the circumstances, your feelings then and whether this meant that you were wanting or were persuaded to go back to Austria?

BR: I never felt that I wanted to go back to Austria. I felt that I was British, very pleased and glad to be British and I wanted to pursue my life in the United Kingdom. My sister, on the other hand, had not become naturalized and had not been able to get a long way in any suitable career, so she decided that she would like to join my parents and return to Vienna. We had a pleasant meeting in the American zone of Austria at a holiday resort,[38] then we parted from my parents and started to make arrangements for my sister to return to Vienna. And I pursued my career as a student in Northumberland.

DT: Were there any complications for your sister to return to the Russian-occupied zone of Vienna?

BR: Not really, because by this time within Vienna proper, the divisions between the different zones had become much freer and my father was now living, I think, in the British zone. All of these zones came to points very close to each other. In any event, by then the occupation forces permitted much local self-government in Vienna.

DT: So you decided to return to Britain, but I understand that you didn't simply pursue your architectural career immediately, that something came in between?

BR: Well, when I got my first degree, an honours degree in architecture, I was then called up to do my National Service as a British citizen. I did my National Service in the Royal Engineers and spent eight or nine months training to be a field engineer. This made me very fit and strong, building bridges and rafts for tanks to go across rivers, demolishing things and making field defences. After eight or nine months, I was called to a War Office selection board and selected for officer training. That sent me first to do an all-arms infantry OCTU (Officer Cadets Training Unit) for some weeks, then subsequently I went to do a much longer Royal Engineers OCTU, at the end of which I was commissioned as a second lieutenant in the Royal Engineers.

DT: I understand that at some point you also received news unexpectedly about your father?

BR: Yes. After the war, my parents had something like six reasonable years with my father able to resume his medical contacts, practices and engagements, and he continued to practise as a very well known skin and venereal specialist in the city. They were able to get a proper flat to live in and for a while my sister lived with them. Then my sister married and had her own family.[39] She became the resource centre manager and chief librarian at the American International School in Vienna, and my father regained his place in the different institutions of which he had been a member before the Nazi time.[40]

I had finished my five-year architecture course and by this time had completed rather more than a year of my National Service. As a subaltern in the Royal Engineers, I was taking part in a night scheme somewhere in the Home Counties. I had just finished digging a weapons pit to put a mortar in when the moonlight shone on two shining boots at the top of the excavation. And there was a military policeman saying, "Which one of you is Mr Rosner? The adjutant wants you." I thought, "My word! What on earth have I done wrong now?" Anyway I climbed out and went to see the adjutant.

"Do you have family living in Austria?" he asked, and I said, "Well, yes, I do as it happens: my father, mother and sister." And he said, "Well, it has been reported to British army, Vienna, and to British army, Austria – by your mother, I think – that your father has died. I have authority to send you on five days' leave to go and bury him. I'm sorry about this tragic news, but if you hand in your bedding and put on your best battle dress, I'll finish the administrative work to issue you with a leave pass and travel warrant. We'll get transport to the railway station to get you on the first train to Liverpool Street. You'll go by military ship to the Hook of Holland and join one of the five military trains that leave the Hook each morning. That will go as far as Klagenfurt, where you'll spend a night in the mess. They'll equip you with documentation to go through the Russian zone and you'll be able to bury your father in a proper manner and return here."

So I had the extraordinary and for me very poignant experience of returning to Vienna in Her Majesty's uniform to bury my father. And I remember on that occasion, after the event, going to pay my respects to what was then only a temporary memorial to the people who had died in the Gestapo headquarters. The building itself had been destroyed. I remember drawing myself up, paying my respects and saying to myself, "And what have you got to say to yourself, Bob?" Having learnt some builders' language as an architectural student, all I could think of was, "Well, the buggers didn't get us all." Not a great philosophical point, but true.

DT: So they didn't get you all. And in a sense your family seems to have been quite exceptional in that four members survived. I wonder if you could just briefly outline what happened to members of the wider family, because your mother's side was Catholic and your father's Jewish?

BR: The Catholic side, my mother's family, had no special experiences other than those of other people in Austria. As I mentioned earlier, Maria, one of my mother's younger sisters, was a very good administrator and found herself put in charge of a large company which the Nazis had taken over or stolen from a Jewish proprietor. This gave her considerable facilities to aid my parents when they were in hiding because she was a powerful person in charge of a powerful company.

On my father's side, the Jewish side of the family, in 1939 they all lived in Poland. My father's father, my grandfather,[41] lived there; my auntie, my father's sister,[42] her husband[43] and their two children all lived near Krakow. My auntie taught English at Breslau University, her husband was a lawyer and my grandfather lived nearby. My auntie's children in 1939 were a 17-year-old boy,[44] who was not academically very bright but a great athlete and sportsman (water polo, skiing and dinghy sailing) and a girl who was about 15 years old,[45] still at school.

When the Germans marched into Poland, my grandfather died within a day or two. The rest of the family were very wisely able to move into the Russian sector of the divided Poland, where they were all immediately jailed. The son of the family immediately disappeared and was not heard of for some years. My uncle, my auntie and my female cousin all found themselves eventually shipped into the Soviet Gulag and finished up at a logging camp near a place called Bokhan on the borders of China.[46]

During the first year of that camp, my uncle died – he wasn't able to cope physically with things – but my auntie and female cousin survived for several years. One day several years later, after a reasonable day (that is, nobody had broken legs or arms through the logging, they had some food to eat and the weather was reasonable) as they were being marched back to the camp, there was quite an animated conversation going on in the ranks of the prisoners. There were occasional jokes, laughter and so on. My auntie was utterly amazed to hear somebody whistling 'My bonny lies over the ocean.' As an English teacher she had known this popular song – it was a little bit of English that she had taught her son and daughter.

My auntie worked her way through the ranks until she was walking next to the fellow who was whistling and she said, "Look, how come here on the borders of China I hear you whistling an English song, 'My bonny lies over the ocean'?" He was a well-built, strong young man and he said, "Well, you see, I was in a Soviet assault unit with a lunatic Pole who was forever bloody well singing this song or whistling it." That's how my auntie discovered that her son had been alive at least a few months before. Not only that, but she learnt that he was now a major in the Soviet army and had been decorated with the Order of Lenin.

When they got back to camp, she went to the administration and said she wished to send a congratulatory note to her son, who was in that particular assault unit. They gave her a piece of paper and a pencil, and she wrote a note congratulating him on his award and wishing him well, expecting all of this to go into the waste paper basket. Nothing was heard for a few months, but then one day she was called to the camp administration. On a table there were two large sacks of food. My aunt was told that she and her daughter must go to the stores and equip themselves with the very best clothes that they could find because they were going on a long journey. They were being released from the camp and issued with a *laissez-passer* and open travel warrant, so that when they stepped out of the camp, they could use whatever resources were available to help them on their journey back home to Krakow.

DT: And I understand that by various means, they eventually got back and were able to make contact with the son?

BR: It was a fantastic journey, as you might imagine, several thousand miles. They started off with various camel trains, camel trolleys, camel sledges and so on, and then a lot of horse-drawn facilities. Occasionally, they would get lifts on military or other transport, but most of their successful travelling was by river. They had the experience of every conceivable form of river traffic – a lot of rafting, a lot of ferries and steamboats, and every possible kind of river vessel. Their journey took place largely across devastated territory and took many months. During that journey, there were large periods when they were only a few miles inside the Soviet front fighting the Nazi army; and they were very fortunate to be able to find food and some kind of transportation. Eventually they did get back to Krakow, just a very short time after the Soviets had pushed the Germans out of that part of Poland. Not only did they manage to find their way back to Krakow, but they also discovered that the son was now Deputy Chief of Police, a very powerful man indeed and, of course, a senior KGB person. He was therefore easily able to provide them with somewhere to live and with ration cards. And that's how they survived the war. An amazing story.

DT: That's the second amazing story in your family. Looking back, you've mentioned to us in builders' language your feelings when you were back in Vienna. Some people have said, having survived the Holocaust in one way or another, that they've been subject to a feeling of guilt that they did survive. Has that ever been your feeling at all?

BR: I've often felt this. I've felt, "Why me?" And it's not a question of getting an answer to "Why me?" It's a question of what happened to everyone. As a *Kindertransportee*, I was one of a lucky, almost 10,000 young people who came to this country. The Germans murdered, industrially murdered, 1.5 million young children. I was one of a tiny, tiny proportion of lucky ones. I'm not sure that 'guilt' is the right word. I used only to feel angry about the circumstances. Now that I'm an older man, more frail and vulnerable, it makes me feel very tearful.

DT: Just to conclude your story, when you came out of the army, you were able to take up your career as a successful architect?

BR: Yes, immediately on demobilization I got myself a job with a prestigious architectural and town-planning office in London. I worked for several years in London for Sir Frederick Gibberd.[47] During that period I also started the second year of an evening course in town planning at Regent Street Polytechnic, because I had taken one year of a town planning evening course at university. Secondly, I also started teaching part-time, one evening a week, 'Building Construction IV', also at Regent Street Polytechnic. So I continued some connection with the academic world. I eventually got an 'exhibition', a scholarship to enable me to do a postgraduate university course in landscape design. So after some years, I finished my job in London and went back up to Tyneside to do a full-time course in landscape design. I managed to complete this and became a qualified landscape designer. Then I took a job with the planning department of Northumberland County Council, where I worked as one of the senior members of staff for a few years.

I also met my wife (my first wife) and got married up there, and subsequently I answered an advertisement for someone to start an office for some architects from the south of England,[48] who wanted to have a northern office at Hull. I got the job and started work for these architects who were based in St Albans and Colchester, and now had a third branch up in Hull. That was very good training for me. I learnt how to do practically everything.

I did that job for somewhat over three years and had meanwhile got a diploma in town planning, with distinction. Then I was offered a very good academic job at Leeds, so for three years I went to Leeds where I became senior lecturer in town planning. Whilst I was there, a friend of mine[49] approached me to ask whether I was interested in starting an architectural and town planning practice with him. I agreed and eventually, working from our homes, we started in private practice. That resulted in some 27 years of successful private practice as architects, town planners and landscape designers, always with some offices in the north of England and a principal administrative office in Hull. I felt that since this part of the world had gifted me my life, I wanted to give some immediate return when that was possible. But we had other offices elsewhere and we were lucky enough to be successful.

We did work overseas as well as in this country and I found the world of architecture, town planning and landscape design very rewarding. I think that I was able to return something in practical terms to UK society because, apart from designing good buildings (I hope) around this country, the work which I did overseas was mostly in the employ of British contractors on overseas contracts. I felt I was able to be part of the sharp end of British ingenuity, British enterprise and British skill. I was responsible for jobs in places as strange as Burma, Egypt, West Africa and elsewhere overseas, and I always felt that I was at the sharp end of British technology and enterprise and I was doing my bit there for my new country.

DT: From what you have just said, it suggests that not only do you have an official document that declares you are a naturalized British citizen, but that emotionally, too, you belong here. Would that be a fair summary?

BR: I feel entirely British. I'm not a Jew who happens to be in Britain. I'm British and happen to be Jewish.

DT: Do you have any feelings at all for Austria and Vienna?

BR: I've been back many times. I find it is possible for me to go there without continually thinking about what the grandparents of these people

I see were doing to people I knew when I was a kid. And Vienna is perhaps the cultural peak of experience in the world. If you're interested in music, art, opera or the theatre, it's a wonderful place to visit. And I've done that several times. My first wife[50] unfortunately died some years ago in tragic circumstances and I'm now fortunate enough to have found and married a second wife,[51] who for me is my whole world.

DT: Could I finally ask you to sum up anything that your remarkable experiences have taught you, any sort of outlook on life that you have developed out of all of this?

BR: What life does to you in many ways is not so important because you can't regulate it. But what you do with life, that is important because that's entirely up to you. I would like just to mention a couple of thoughts which are often in my mind. Two of these are quotations from other people. The first one is, "Salvation lies in acknowledging our weaknesses and recognizing and loving the uniqueness of every individual."[52] Secondly, "True democracy begins with free confession of our sins, and all real unity commences with a consciousness of differences."[53] Freedom does not come from the avoidance of obligation or the evasion of responsibility. Faced with the immense wickedness and bestiality of some people, which can often be accompanied by immense physical and financial resources, it pays the rest of us to be aware and alert to support those seeking justice.

DT: Thank you very much, Bob.

Notes

1. Rudolf Rosner (1887-1955).
2. Sieglinde (Lilly) Rosner, née Stiasny (1899-1972).
3. Renate Rosner (b. 1926).
4. Wipplingerstrasse 6.
5. Bielitz or Bielsko (now Bielsko-Biala) in southern Poland, about 40 miles south-west of Krakow, on the river Biala.
6. Primarius Dr Rosner was *Consiliar-Facharzt der Wiener Krankenkasse für Industrie und Angestellte* (Consultant Specialist to the Viennese Health and Social Security Insurance Scheme). In addition to private work at his consulting rooms in Wipplingerstrasse, he also carried out research at the *Universitätsklinik für Haut- und Geschlechtskrankheiten* and published the results in various medical journals.
7. In Vienna Bob attended a well-known Catholic school in the First District. It is not without irony that he recalls one year playing the part of Mary in the annual nativity play.
8. It is in fact almost certain that giving Trépol and small doses of malaria were separate or alternative treatments.
9. The Austrian Chancellor Engelbert Dollfuss was assassinated on 25 July 1934 during an attempted National Socialist *putsch*.
10. An outstanding example of this social housing was the Karl-Marx-Hof, designed by Karl Ehn, built in 1930 and still standing today.
11. The *Anschluss* was effected when German troops crossed the border on 12 March 1938.
12. Bob can no longer remember the name of the school, but remembers it was in the Börsegasse.
13. The *Kristallnacht* or *Reichspogromnacht* from 9-10 November 1938.
14. The greengrocer Tobias, aka Edward or Teddy, Tallerman (1901-1980) was also a native of Hull. He lived with his wife Faye and daughter Mona over the shop.
15. Joseph Leopold (Leo) Schultz (1900-1991) was a native of Hull. For many years he was a member of the city council there and alderman from 1962 to 1974. A life-long Socialist, he gained widespread respect, but also the hostility of a minority, for his insistence on absolute probity in public life. He was awarded the OBE in 1945 and knighted in 1966.

16. Lionel Schultz, b. 1931. After graduating as a mining engineer, he became senior safety and ventilation officer for the National Coal Board.

17. A Rover.

18. Kate (Kitty) Schultz, née Pickersgill (1902-1975).

19. A council house on the North Hull Estate at 18 Etton Grove. Following war damage, the terrace was replaced by semi-detached houses.

20. Dr Robert Haas came originally from Dahn, Rheinland-Pfalz.

21. 'Elbow grease' is a humorous expression for energetic work, especially vigorous rubbing; 'strap oil' is slang for flogging with a strap. So I was being sent to buy non-existent goods – and possibly to receive unpleasant treatment.

22. Renate Rosner attended Eastfield Road School before moving to the College of Commerce in Brunswick Avenue.

23. The aviator Amy Johnson (1903-1941).

24. The school changed its name from Boulevard Secondary School to Kingston High School when it moved to new premises in Pickering Road, Hull, in 1939.

25. These were air-raid shelters with a curved roof and consisted of one room. They were made of concrete-clad corrugated steel sheeting, erected on a partially sunken reinforced concrete floor slab. They derived their name from the fact that they were officially adopted when Sir John Anderson was Home Secretary (1939-1940).

26. On the basis of this early promotion of Anderson shelters, which is reckoned to have saved thousands of lives, Leo Schultz was described in the press as the 'Prince of Wonderland'.

27. Elizabeth Mary DeVelling was herself a former pupil of Boulevard Secondary School between 1907 and 1917. She returned to the school as a teacher in the early 1920s and retired from Kingston High School in 1961.

28. The teacher was Mr Miles Lerner, who rejoined the staff in 1946.

29. Dr William Cameron Walker (1896-1978) was headmaster of the school from 1938 until his retirement in 1961.

30. Sydney Herbert Smith (1885-1984), Member of Hull City Council from 1927 to 1968 and Labour Member of Parliament for Hull South-West from 1945-1950.

31. Mrs Lucy Middleton, née Cox (1894-1983), was Labour Member of Parliament for Plymouth Sutton between 1945 and 1951. During the war she had attempted to maintain links with German émigrés and after the war, sought among other things to build friendships with the German people who were anxious to rebuild their shattered towns.

32. Maria Stiasny (dates unknown).

33. Viktor Karl Mayerhofer (1882-1953).

34. Böheimkirchen, near St. Pölten in Lower Austria.

35. Rully or rulley, a local dialect word for a flat four-wheeled cart.

36. To judge from visits to Vienna by horse and cart that Viktor Mayerhofer undertook in the 1920s, the journey would have lasted about ten hours.

37. According to members of the Mayerhofer family, he transported provisions in a rucksack, together with dog food by way of camouflage.

38. Thumersbach near Zell am See.

39. Frau Renate C. Jeschaunig still lives in Vienna.

40. He lived and had his private consulting rooms at Neutorgasse 12 in the First District. He also worked at the Sophienspital, the Börseplatz Ambulatorium and for the Wiener Gebietskrankenkasse.

41. Salomon Rosner (date of birth unknown; died during the German attack on Poland in 1939).

42. Hilda Glücksman (1889-c1970). The surname was later sovietized to Gruda.

43. Sigmund Glücksman (dates unknown) was a Social Democrat member of Bielitz town council as well as a solicitor.

44. Konrad Glücksman/Gruda (precise dates unknown), who subsequently became a writer and television personality.

45. Ruth (Uta) Glücksman/Gruda (precise dates unknown).

46. Bokhan lies not far from Irkutsk, Lake Baikal and the Mongolian border.

47. Sir Frederick Ernest Gibberd (1908-1984), architect and town planner. The offices were in Percy Street, off Tottenham Court Road.

48. Taylor & Hunt.

49. Arnold C. Parker.

50. Freda Kathleen (Kaye) Rosner, née Smith (1926-2000).

51. Olive L. Rosner, formerly Ferguson.

52. Source of quotation unknown.

53. Source of quotation uncertain, possibly from W.H. Auden.

Illustrations

The Rosner family with friends, 1937.

Poster advertising antisemitic exhibition at one of Vienna's principal railway stations, August 1938.

Bob's passport with the obligatory false name 'Israel' and the capital J for Jude *(Jew).*

With guardians Kitty and Leo, first day in England, 1939.

Bob with his foster brother Lionel, 1939.

School prefects, Kingston High School, 1947. Bob is third from left, back row.

With his guardians on graduation day.

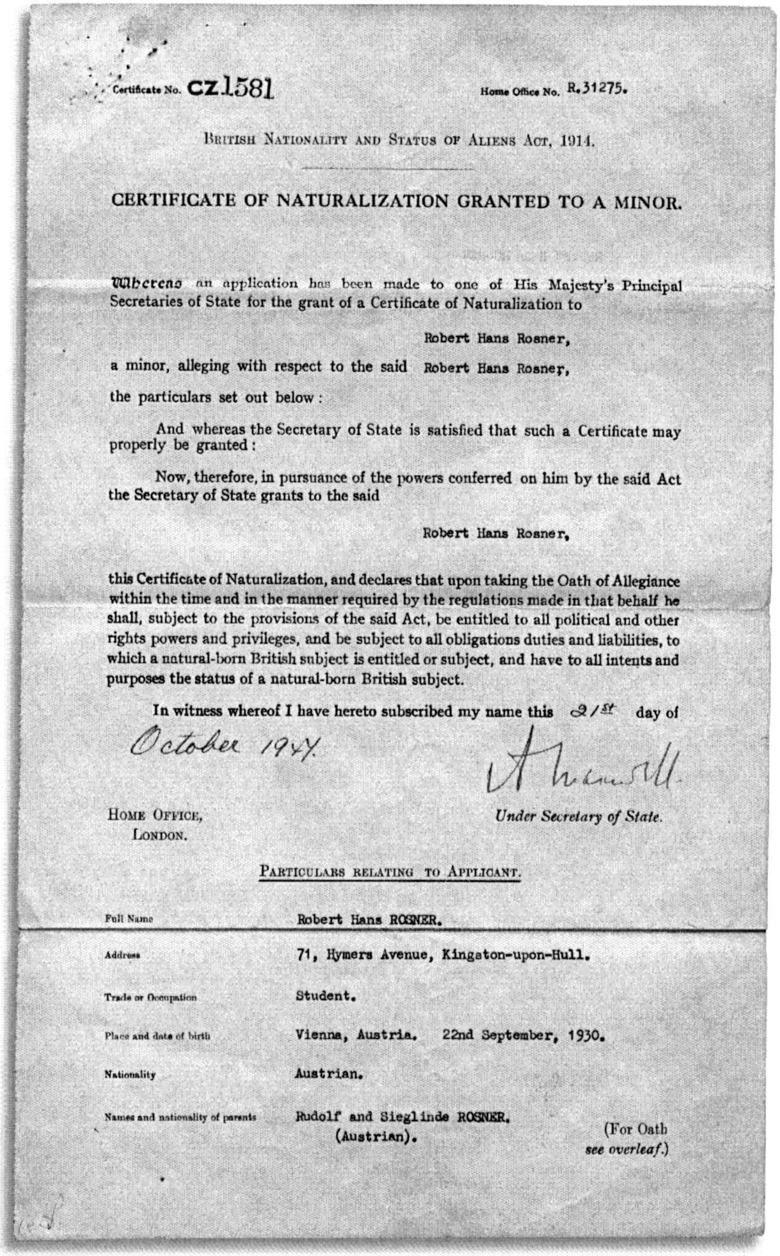

Certificate No. CZ1581 Home Office No. R.31275.

British Nationality and Status of Aliens Act, 1914.

CERTIFICATE OF NATURALIZATION GRANTED TO A MINOR.

Whereas an application has been made to one of His Majesty's Principal Secretaries of State for the grant of a Certificate of Naturalization to

Robert Hans Rosner,

a minor, alleging with respect to the said Robert Hans Rosner,

the particulars set out below:

And whereas the Secretary of State is satisfied that such a Certificate may properly be granted:

Now, therefore, in pursuance of the powers conferred on him by the said Act the Secretary of State grants to the said

Robert Hans Rosner,

this Certificate of Naturalization, and declares that upon taking the Oath of Allegiance within the time and in the manner required by the regulations made in that behalf he shall, subject to the provisions of the said Act, be entitled to all political and other rights powers and privileges, and be subject to all obligations duties and liabilities, to which a natural-born British subject is entitled or subject, and have to all intents and purposes the status of a natural-born British subject.

In witness whereof I have hereto subscribed my name this 21st day of October 1947.

Home Office, London.

Under Secretary of State.

PARTICULARS RELATING TO APPLICANT.

Full Name	Robert Hans ROSNER.
Address	71, Hymers Avenue, Kingston-upon-Hull.
Trade or Occupation	Student.
Place and date of birth	Vienna, Austria. 22nd September, 1930.
Nationality	Austrian.
Names and nationality of parents	Rudolf and Sieglinde ROSNER. (Austrian).

(For Oath see overleaf.)

Certificate of Naturalization, 1947.

Commissioned Second Lieutenant, Royal Engineers.

At an all-arms infantry Officer Cadets Training Unit. Bob is fourth from left, back row.

Father's burial in Vienna when Bob was an Army of Occupation officer.

Congratulated by HM The Queen at the official opening of the Humber Bridge, 1980.

Toll and administration building, Humber Bridge. This photo, and the following four, all show buildings designed by Bob Rosner.

Interior and exterior of the German Lutheran Church, Hull.

Lock control at the entrance to Hull Marina.

Dove House Hospice, Hull.

Bob and Olive, newly-weds, 2003.

Bob being interviewed, by courtesy of The Journal, *Hull.*